What Is Gratitude?

Draw a fancy line to the missing words that best fit each sentence.

I _____ AND SHOW THANKS TO GOD EVERY DAY!

often

I ____ MY THANKFULNESS AND APPRECIATION WHEN SOMEONE HAS GIVEN ME SOMETHING.

notes

show

I AM HAPPY WITH THE _____ LITTLE THINGS AND NOT ALWAYS LOOKING FOR MORE.

praise

I SAY THANK YOU AS _____ AS I CAN.

I WRITE THANK-YOU _____ TO ALL MY FRIENDS WHO GAVE ME BIRTHDAY GIFTS.

simple

I DO ____ THINGS TO THOSE WHO HAVE BEEN NICE TO ME.

kind

Why Should I?

HOW WOULD YOU FEEL IF YOU GAVE SOMEONE A GIFT AND THEY REPLIED ...?

But I wanted something else.

I DON'T LIKE IT, YOU CAN KEEP IT.

OKAY, GOTTA GO NOW!

Why didn't you give me the bigger one?

What else do you have for me?

That's not a proper gift.

Write in the speech bubble, how you might feel:

Thanks to God

Write down in the shapes some of the things that you're thankful for.

Let's Investigate

Read the stories and match the grateful endings to each one.

Linda's favorite color is purple, so when she received a yellow flower pillow for her birthday, she was a little disappointed.

THESE AREN'T THE ONES THAT I REALLY WANTED, BUT AT LEAST I STILL GOT TO TRADE IN SOME CARDS.

All the kids took a turn to race their wind-up toy cars, but there could be only one winner. And it wasn't Jamie. He came in second place.

COOKING IS NOT MY FAVORITE ACTIVITY, BUT AT LEAST I GET TO FINISH OFF ALL THE TASTY LEFTOVERS.

When Kelly wanted to sign up for school activities, there were none left that she really wanted to do. All her favorite activities were already taken.

I DIDN'T DO TOO BAD FOR MY FIRST TIME RACING, AND THAT MEANS NEXT TIME I CAN ONLY GET BETTER!

Stevie traded some of his favorite cards with Carl at school today. But he didn't get the ones that he was hoping for.

OH WOW! THIS COLOR IS NOT EXACTLY WHAT I LIKE, BUT I'M SO GLAD THAT I GOT SOMETHING THAT I REALLY NEEDED.

Saying "Thank You!"

In how many different ways can you say "Thank you"? Ask your neighbors or friends if they know how to say it in a different language and write it in the papers below.

Blanks Bunny

Find the word in each of the vegetables that does not belong. Write it in a box below, to find the secret message.

- BE TULIP ROSE
- PAPER SCISSOR THANKFUL
- BANANA FOR APPLE
- MOUNTAIN OCEAN WHAT
- YOU PIE CAKE
- SUN ALREADY RAIN
- DOLL PUZZLE HAVE

Help Bunny find the keyword so that he can be grateful too.

Wise Words

Read the Bible verses using the big word in the middle that says "thanks". Then write something in each letter that you're thankful for.

T

GIVE — TO THE LORD, FOR HE IS GOOD. PSALM 107:1

H

GIVE — FOR EVERYTHING TO GOD. EPHESIANS 5:20

A

SING SONGS WITH — IN YOUR HEARTS TO GOD. COLOSSIANS 3:16

N

— BE TO GOD FOR HIS AMAZING GIFT! 2 CORINTHIANS 9:15

K

GIVE — TO THE LORD; CALL UPON HIS NAME. PSALM 105:1

S

LET THE PEACE OF CHRIST RULE IN YOUR HEARTS, AND ALWAYS GIVE — COLOSSIANS 3:15

I WILL SING YOUR PRAISES AND NOT BE SILENT. I WILL GIVE YOU — FOREVER! PSALM 30:12

WHATEVER YOU DO OR SAY, DO EVERYTHING GIVING — TO GOD. COLOSSIANS 3:17

AS YOU COME BEFORE GOD, GIVE HIM — AND PRAISE AND BLESS HIS NAME! PSALM 100:4

I TAKE TIME TO GIVE — TO GOD DURING MY TIME OF PRAYER. PHILEMON 1:4

Celebrate Your Senses

Have you praised God and celebrated the joy of having your five senses? Imagine you didn't have one of them? How would things be different for you? Read the little prayers, and match the word in BOLD letters to the picture on the right.

- DEAR GOD, THANK YOU FOR MY **EYES**. I LIKE TO LOOK AT THE BEAUTIFUL BLUE SKY.
- THANK YOU FOR GIVING ME **EARS**. MY FAVORITE SOUND IS BIRDS SINGING.
- THANK YOU FOR CREATING SKIN. I REALLY LIKE THE **FEEL** OF MY SOFT BLANKET.
- THANK YOU FOR MY **TONGUE** AND THE TASTE OF CHOCOLATE.
- THANK YOU, GOD, FOR GOOD **SMELLS**, ESPECIALLY THE SMELL OF BAKED BREAD.
- THANK YOU, GOD, FOR ALL MY FIVE **SENSES** THAT HELP ME TO ENJOY LIFE.

Ollie's Lessons

THE LEAF

Leaves are like tiny factories that make food for the tree. Leaves give us shade, they give us oxygen, they help moisturize the ground after they fall. But one very important job the leaves have is to create nourishment for the fruit. If there were no leaves, we would have no fruit.

Now pretend that you are like a fruit and every time someone says something nice to you, thanks you or shows their appreciation, it's adding one more leaf to the tree, to help you grow into a big and delicious fruit.

? DID YOU KNOW? IT TAKES 50 LEAVES TO MAKE ONE APPLE. IT TAKES 12 LEAVES TO MAKE A BUNCH OF BANANAS. IT TAKES GENERALLY MORE THAN 30 LEAVES TO MAKE MANY OTHER FRUITS.

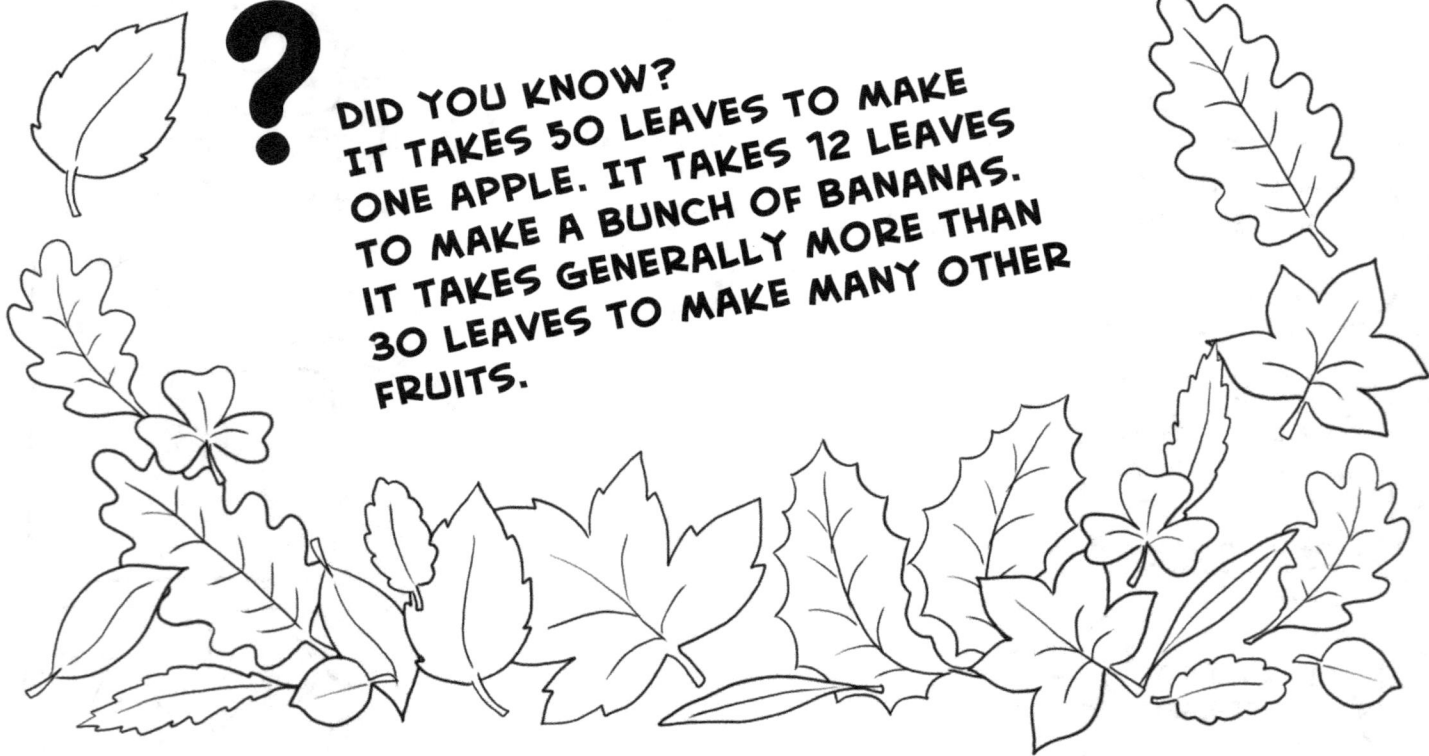

Color the matching leaves. Find the odd one out that doesn't have a matching pair.

Try it Out!

1. You can make your own gratitude tree. Create the trunk and branches of a tree by using brown craft paper and hang it on a door or wall. Cut out paper leaves to stick to your tree.

2. Each day write something that you are thankful for on a leaf and tape it to the tree. You can write as many as you can think of, but don't repeat any.

3. Every time you get 10 leaves on the tree, add a fruit-shaped cutout from red or orange paper.

4. Try this out for one week and see how many fruits you've grown on your tree and also how it feels to practice gratitude.

You will need:
- large sheets of colored papers (red, green and brown)
- a pen or marker
- glue
- scissors

Write down 4 things that come to mind that you want to thank God for.

Illustrate a Bible Story

(From 1 Samuel 1-2)

Read this Bible story and have fun drawing it.

HANNAH TRIED HARD TO BE THANKFUL, BUT IT WAS DIFFICULT FOR HER BECAUSE SHE WAS OFTEN VERY SAD THAT SHE DIDN'T HAVE A CHILD. ONE EVENING, HANNAH WENT TO THE TEMPLE TO PRAY.

SHE TOLD GOD ABOUT HER SADNESS AND ABOUT HER WISH TO HAVE A CHILD. "DEAR GOD, IF YOU GIVE ME A SON, I PROMISE THAT I WILL LET HIM SERVE YOU," SHE SAID.

EARLY THE NEXT MORNING SHE WORSHIPED AND THANKED GOD. HER HEART WAS FILLED WITH JOY AND GRATEFULNESS BECAUSE SHE KNEW THAT GOD HAD HEARD HER PRAYER.

A LITTLE WHILE LATER, A GREAT THING HAPPENED! GOD REMEMBERED HANNAH'S PRAYER AND GAVE HER A SON, AND SHE NAMED HIM SAMUEL.

Story Application

I'M ALLIE. I'M READY TO HELP YOU APPLY GOD'S WORD TO YOUR OWN LIFE STORY.

God KNOWS what's BEST and there's always a GOOD reason why He doesn't answer ALL our prayers or not right away. But we can still THANK Him and be GRATEFUL for all the things He has already given us and BLESSED us with.

When Samuel was old enough, Hannah went back to the temple and told the priest that she was letting Samuel live at the temple, so that he could learn to become one of God's helpers. That was her special way of saying "THANK YOU" to God.

Everyone has different ways of showing their thanks and gratitude. Write down some of the things that you like to do, to show God that you're grateful for the things He does?

1.
2.
3.
4.

Find Your Way

Help the boy to find gratefulness as he goes through the maze.
What are some things that can help you stay cheerful even if things don't go your way?

MAX SO LOOKED FORWARD TO PLAYING WITH HIS FRIEND TODAY, BUT THINGS DIDN'T QUITE WORK OUT THAT WAY.

BUT HE'S GRATEFUL THAT HE HAD TIME WITH HIS FRIEND YESTERDAY, AND THAT THEY GOT TO DO LOTS OF FUN THINGS TOGETHER.

Coloring Page

GOD BLESSED HANNAH WITH A SON. SHE THANKED AND WORSHIPED GOD OVER AND OVER AGAIN. "I PRAISE YOU, GOD! YOU ARE GREAT! YOU ARE AWESOME!" SHE SAID.

Intentionally blank

Intentionally blank

Find out How

There are many different ways to show your gratefulness to God and others around you, but it can start with one very simple way. Find out how!

Color all the boxes with a dot RED. Color all the boxes with a triangle YELLOW, and find the secret message.

God Is Good

Read the story by using the pictures to help you.

"Isn't the 🌱 lovely? Jesus makes the 🌱 green," 👩 told her little 👦.
"Why does Jesus make the 🌱 green?" asked the 👦. "Because He is 👍,"
👩 said. "He also made the ☁️ blue, the 🌼 yellow, your 🐱 brown
and the 🍎 red." "Why did Jesus make them those colors," asked the 👦.
"Well," his 👩 explained, "you wouldn't like to have a black ☀️ or blue 🌱
or brown 🌼 or a green 🐱, would you?" Everything God has made in the
🌍 shows how 👍 He is. When the ☀️ starts to shine through the ☁️
on a cold day, we say, "How 👍 the ☀️ feels." But then when the ☀️ gets
too hot and ☁️ cover it and bring 🌧️ to cool things down, we say, "How
👍 the 🌧️ is." God gives us the ☀️ and the 🌧️. Let us be grateful and give
thanks for each thing God does. Remember, God is all 👍!

17

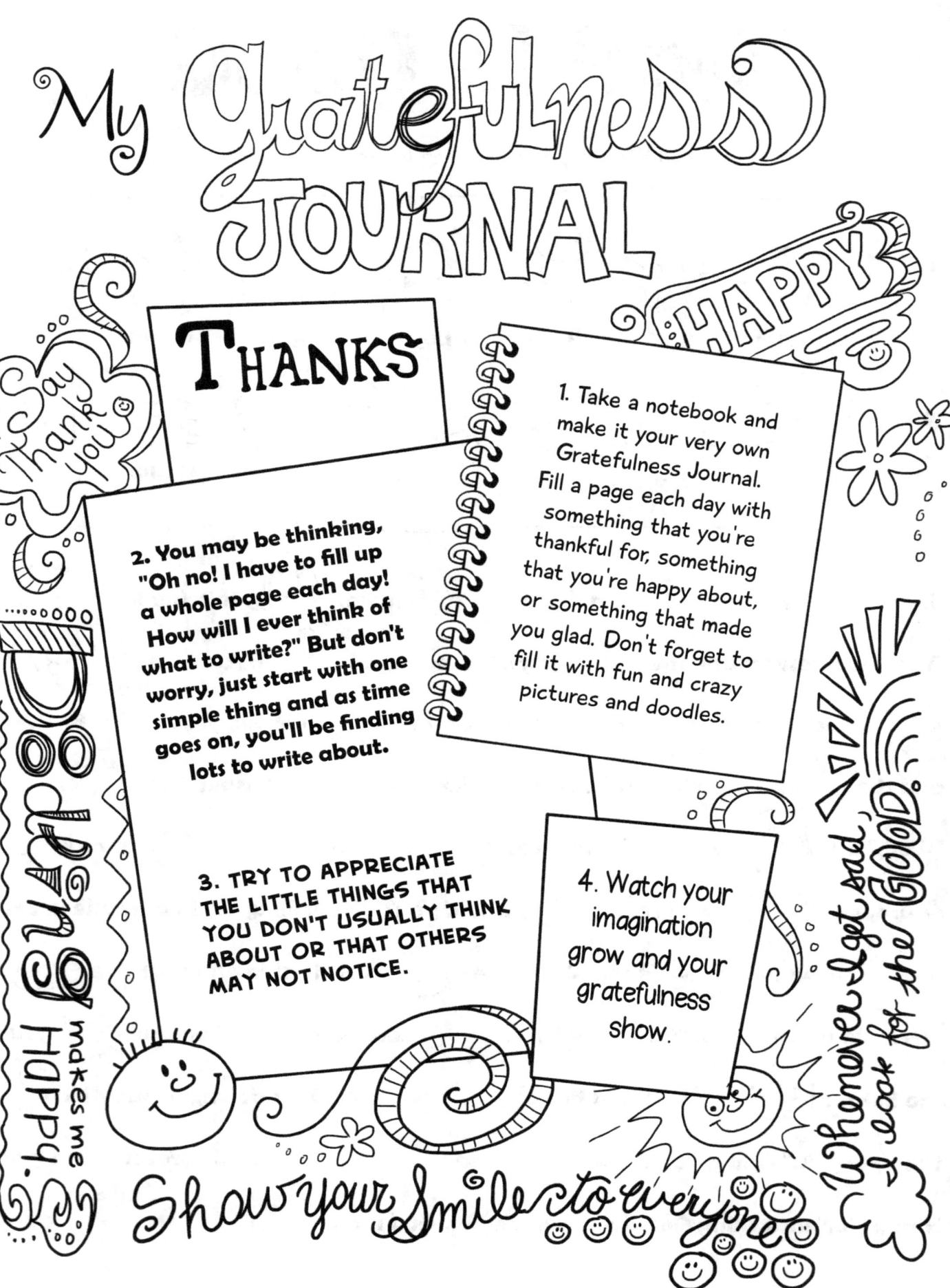

Rhyme a Praise

Color the two boxes that rhyme together in the same color.

LOOK AT ALL THE GREAT THINGS GOD HAS DONE.

GOD LOVES TO RECEIVE OUR PRAISES AND "THANK YOU'S".

I WANT TO COUNT MY BLESSINGS EACH DAY,

I GIVE HONOR AND PRAISE TO GOD FOR CARING FOR ME.

LET'S SHOW HIM OUR GRATITUDE IN THE WORDS WE USE.

LET'S REMEMBER TO THANK HIM FOR EACH ONE.

EVERYONE APPRECIATES THANKS, DON'T YOU AGREE?

AND KEEP A THANKFUL HEART IN ALL I DO AND SAY.

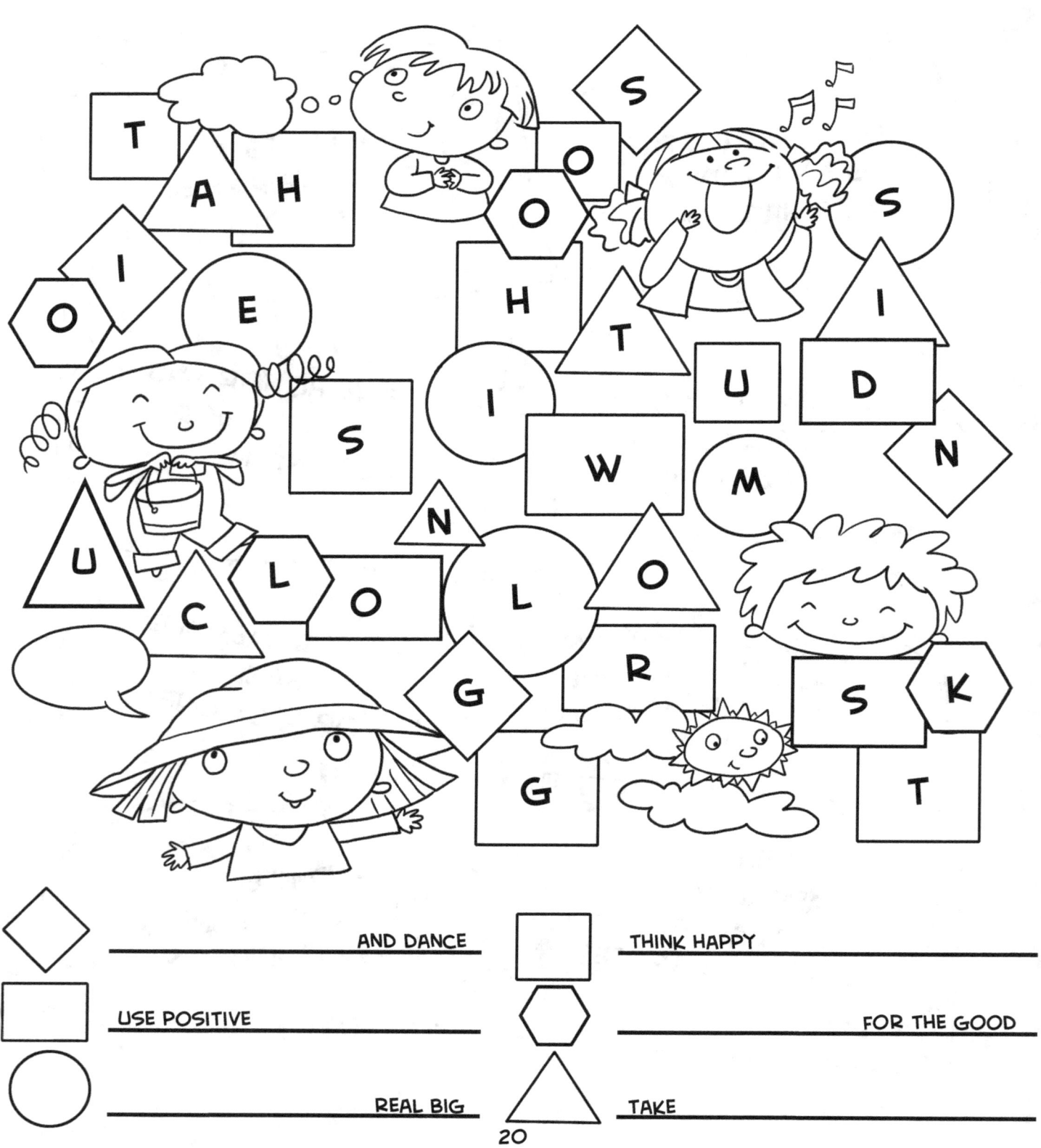

Road to Progress

It helps to have a plan when you want to start a new habit and make progress. List some ways that you can be more grateful.

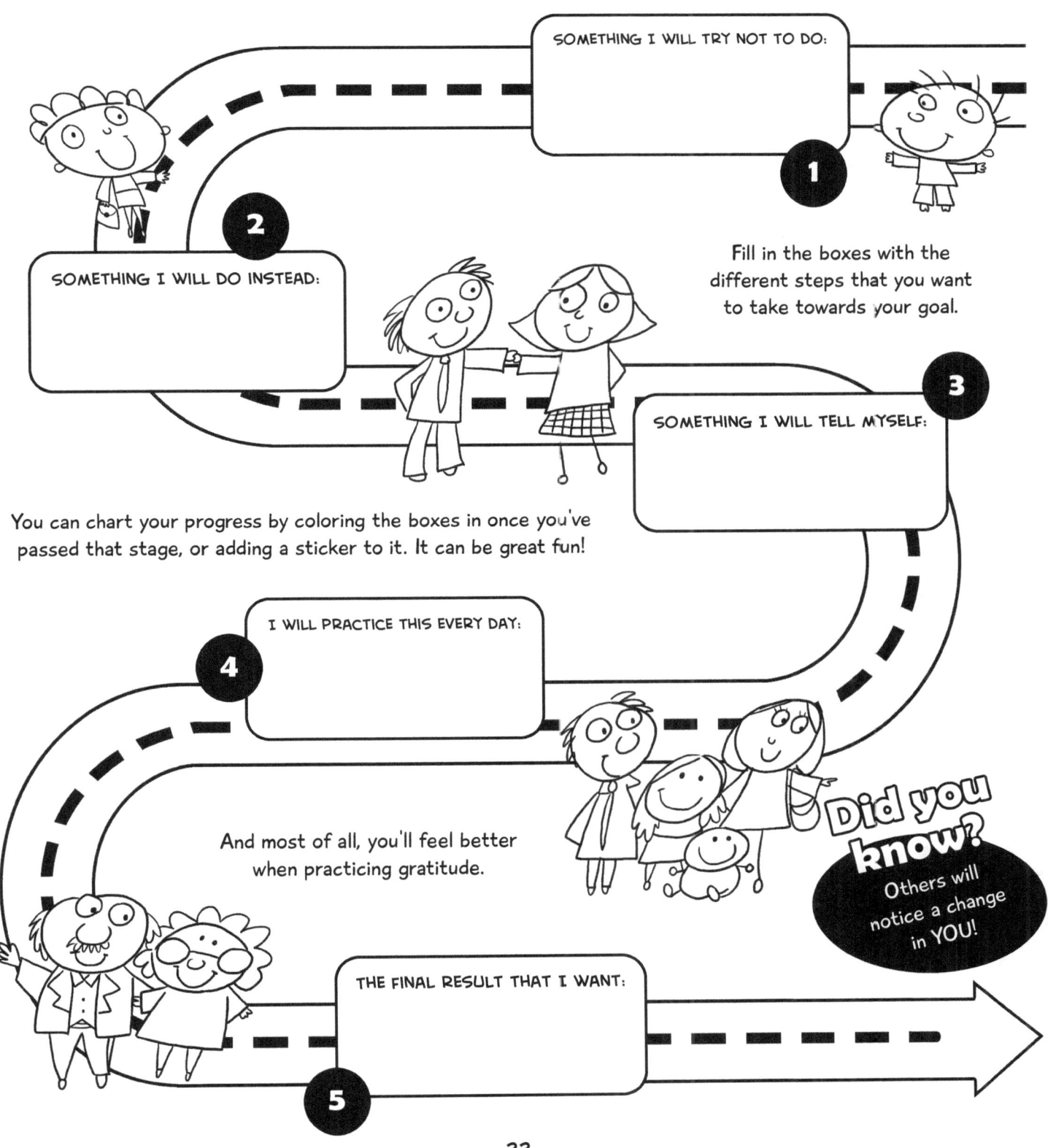

SOMETHING I WILL TRY NOT TO DO:

1

Fill in the boxes with the different steps that you want to take towards your goal.

2

SOMETHING I WILL DO INSTEAD:

3

SOMETHING I WILL TELL MYSELF:

You can chart your progress by coloring the boxes in once you've passed that stage, or adding a sticker to it. It can be great fun!

4

I WILL PRACTICE THIS EVERY DAY:

And most of all, you'll feel better when practicing gratitude.

Did you know? Others will notice a change in YOU!

THE FINAL RESULT THAT I WANT:

5

Intentionally blank

Play and Do

Try out these simple exercises or games to help you practice gratitude.

1. Decorate a piece of paper and write a "thank you" note to someone you are grateful for.

   Explain how you are thankful for them and draw a picture of how it made you feel.

2. Get a die and roll it. The number rolled is the amount of things to thank God for.

   Now try with a second die and glue a different color paper on each of the 6 sides. Roll both dice and thank God for the number of things on the dice you can think of that is the same color as on the dice.

3. Write out the word GRATITUDE at the top of your paper. Below the "G", write things that you are thankful for that begin with that letter. For example: guitars, grandpa. Continue writing words for each letter of "GRATITUDE".

4. Use a light-weight ball and toss it around to each other. Every time you catch it, appreciate someone or something. Then toss it to the next player. Have as many goes as you like, till everyone has had plenty of turns to show their gratitude and thankfulness and had a chance to share it with everyone else too.

Flip and Flop

Gratitude is showing thanks and appreciation for even the small and unimportant things!

Prayer Time

Check out what the Bible has to say about our times in prayer. Circle all the words you find below.

```
H I S P D T B P C E G J S X E T P F
Q A N D T S X Y J P F Q Q Q N C I Y
X B E H B P W C M R V C B W I T H S
P R A I S E C E E E D N B L E S S R
B C W H T H A N K S G I V I N G D C
J I T W W S B R F E F R U B I N T O
B S U J H V T N R N F O R Y L U G M
W B Y O E A Y A H C Q V H N K E M E
F B A T H T Z M O E F M J I Y O S O
H I S Y X C T E O G O O D M C I X S
```

COME INTO HIS PRESENCE WITH THANKSGIVING AND PRAISE. BLESS HIS NAME FOR HE IS GOOD.

Fill in the blanks to personalize this prayer and make it your very own.

Dear God,

I give You thanks because You are good and You are _____.
Thank You for giving me _____.
Sometimes I am tempted to complain about _____.
Please help me to find ways to praise You, even when I am feeling _____.
Help me to be joyful even though I _____.
Help me to notice the good and _____.

In Jesus' name. Amen.

Answer Sheet

What Is Gratitude? - Page 1

I **praise** and show thanks to God every day!
I **show** my thankfulness and appreciation when someone has given me something.
I am happy with the **simple** little things and not always looking for more.
I write thank-you **notes** to all my friends who gave me birthday gifts.
I say thank you as **often** as I can.
I do **kind** things to those who have been nice to me.

Let's Investigate - Page 4

- Linda's favorite color is purple, so when she received a yellow flower pillow for her birthday, she was a little disappointed. → Oh wow! This color is not exactly what I like, but I'm so glad that I got something that I really needed.

- All the kids took a turn to race their wind-up toy cars, but there could be only one winner. And it wasn't Jamie. He came in second place. → I didn't do too bad for my first time racing and that means next time I can only get better!

- When Kelly wanted to sign up for the school activities, there were none left that she really wanted to do. All her favorite activities were already taken. → Cooking is not my favorite activity, but at least I get to finish off all the tasty leftovers.

- Stevie traded some of his favorite cards with Carl at school today. But he didn't get the ones that he was hoping for. → These aren't the ones that I really wanted, but at least I still got to trade in some cards.

Saying "Thank you!" - Page 5

Here are some examples of "thank you" in other languages:

Dankie (Afrikaans)
Obrigado (Portuguese)
Gracias (Spanish)
Merci (French)

Blanks Bunny - Page 7

The secret message is: *Be thankful for what you already have.*

Celebrate Your Senses - Page 9

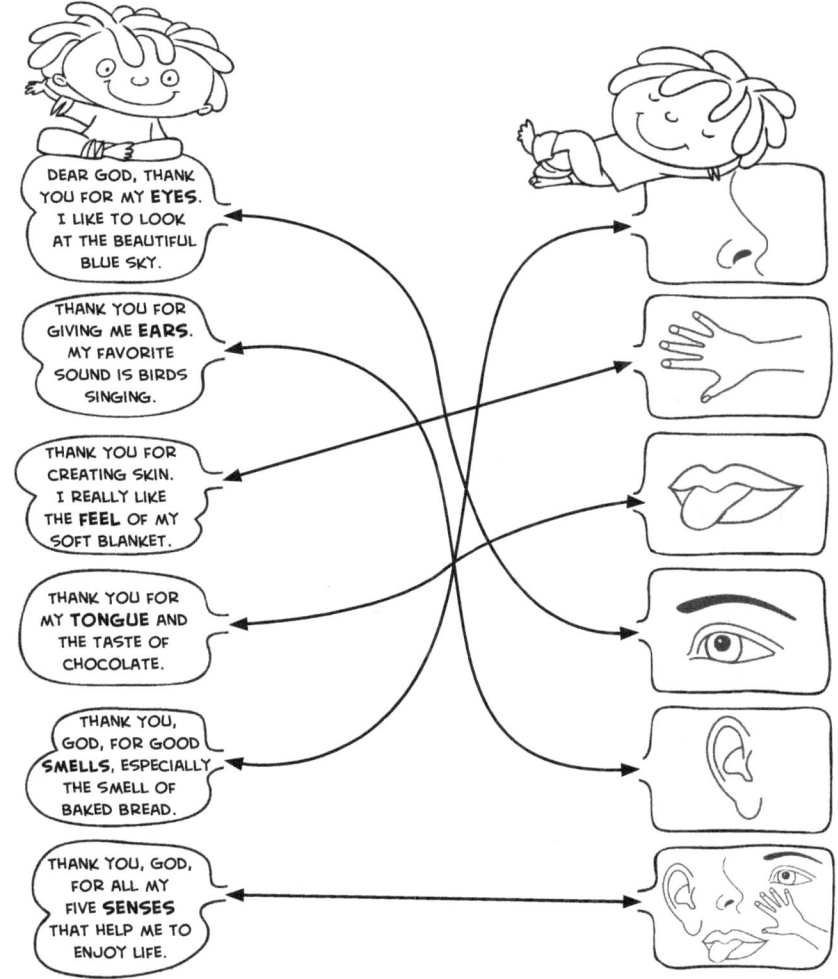

Ollie's Lessons - Page 10

The odd leaf that doesn't have a matching pair is:

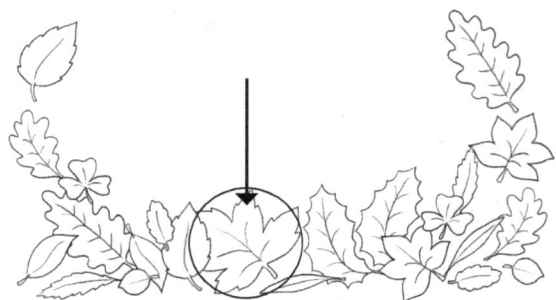

Find Your Way - Page 14

Find out How - Page 16

The secret message is: *Say thank you*

Rhyme a Praise - Page 19

Look at all the great things God has done.
Let's remember to thank Him for each one.

I want to count my blessings each day,
and keep a thankful heart in all I do and say.

Let's show Him our gratitude in the words we use.
God loves to receive our praises and "thank you's".

Everyone appreciates thanks, don't you agree?
I give honor and praise to God for caring for me.

Ways to Show Gratitude - Page 20

Sing and dance
Smile real big
Look for the good
Use positive **words**
Think happy **thoughts**
Take **caution**

Prayer Time - Page 24

Here is an example of how you can pray:

Dear God,
   I give You thanks because You are good and You are **powerful**.
   Thank You for giving me **pretty clothes to wear**.
   Sometimes I am tempted to complain about **wanting more toys.**
   Please help me to find ways to praise You, even when I am feeling **jealous about what others have**.
   Help me to be joyful even though **I don't always get what I want**.
   Help me to notice the good and **to be thankful for what I have**.
   In Jesus' name. Amen.

More books from iCharacter.org

Published by iCharacter Limited ®. (Ireland)
Illustrated by Agnes de Bezenac
All Bible verses adapted from the KJV.
www.iCharacter.org

Copyright © 2015 by iCharacter Limited ®. All rights reserved. No part of this book may be reproduced in any form or by any electronic or mechanical means, including information storage and retrieval systems, without written permission from the publisher or author, except in the case of a reviewer, who may quote brief passages embodied in critical articles or in a review.

www.ingramcontent.com/pod-product-compliance
Lightning Source LLC
Chambersburg PA
CBHW081504070526
44586CB00019B/2477